Barrier-Free Travel
DEATH VALLEY
NATIONAL PARK
for Wheelers and Slow Walkers

Candy B. Harrington

PHOTOGRAPHS BY

CHARLES PANNELL

CANDY & CHARLES CREATIVE CONCEPTS

ISBN: 978-0-9985103-7-8

Candy & Charles Creative Concepts
PO Box 278
Ripon, CA 95366-0278

To Charles

Contents

Preface
A Valley of Life

Death Valley is brimming with life, and that's something that the native people innately recognize. The Timbisha Shoshone do not equate their home with death, as they believe the Creator filled the land with all the resources necessary for their comfort and contentment. In fact, they eschew the park's contemporary name, and instead call their homeland Tümpisa — their name for the indigenous red-ochre earth that's believed to strengthen their spirituality.

Death Valley is indeed filled with life, but you have to slow down and look for it. On my last visit I found Salt Creek filled with pupfish, and colorful spring blooms bursting forth alongside the park roads. The ground near the Grapevine Ranger station was literally covered with tiny caterpillars; and let's not even talk about the quail, rabbits and burros I spotted as we wandered through the park.

This living desert is also a land in transition, as Mother Nature is still molding the landscape. You'll see evidence of that transition in the shifting sand dunes and the eroding rock formations in the park. Stop and listen at Devils Golf Course and you'll hear little pops and cracks — that's the sound of billions of tiny salt crystals bursting apart as the heat causes them to expand and contract. And over at Artists Palette the heat also alters the volcanic minerals on the hillside and provides a rainbow of colors.

And although the natural environment is in a constant state of flux, wheelchair-access in the park is on a straightforward upward course, as the powers that be continue to plan and implement access upgrades. From the access improvements at Badwater and Dantes View to the addition of accessible casitas at the Inn at Death Valley, this seemingly desolate environment is actually quite welcoming to wheelchair-users and slow walkers.

And that's the main reason that I wrote this book — to dispel the myth that Death Valley National Park is an inhospitable environment for wheelchair-users and slow walkers; and to give folks the tools and information they need to plan an accessible visit.

Part of that planning involves getting to the park, which is why I included some attractions and worthwhile stops in the surrounding communities. Like many national park trips, a Death Valley visit is usually a road trip, and there are some fun and accessible things to see along the way. As they say, getting there is half the fun.

Once you arrive though, you'll definitely want to stay in the park, which is why I've included photos and access details about all the in-park lodging options. Rest assured we spent a good deal of time inspecting and photographing the accessible rooms, so you can make an appropriate choice.

Of course access upgrades are continually added to the park trails and facilities, and when they are I will also include these updates on www.BarrierFreeDeathValley.com. And if you happen upon a new addition, let me know so I can share it with everybody.

Oh and here's an interesting Death Valley tidbit for my grammatically inclined friends. You will probably notice that some site names – like Artists Drive, Dantes View and Devils Golf Course – lack the apostrophes to make them grammatically correct. That's because when they were named it wasn't possible to get apostrophes into officially recognized place names. And although it pains me as a writer, I'm sticking with tradition and keeping the grammatically incorrect official names in the book.

In the end, a trip to Death Valley is a glorious adventure. I have fond memories of one girlfriends getaway Death Valley adventure in particular. We had a heck of a time getting the gang together because of our busy schedules, and we ended up slating our Death Valley campout for late May. The temperatures topped 120 degrees during those fateful days, but we persevered and drank copious amount of water. We were the only people in the Stovepipe Wells Campground, and although the bartender at the Badwater Saloon called us "those crazy city girls", I like to think we were trendsetters. Today folks flock to Death Valley in the summer, just to experience those same extreme temperatures. We had a great time that May — we even got invited to an employee party — and we most certainly made a lot of memories.

I'm sure you'll have an equally grand — and accessible — Death Valley adventure of your own. So start packing, and have a great trip. And let me know how it goes.

Candy Harrington
candy@EmergingHorizons.com
www.CandyHarrington.com
www.EmergingHorizons.com
Facebook: Candy Harrington
Twitter: Candy B. Harrington
Pinterest: Candy Harrington

Admission, Reservations and Park Passes

Hells Gate picnic area with fee machine

Admission Fees

The admission fee to Death Valley National Park is $30 per car. There are no entrance kiosks at the park, but the fee can be paid at a visitor center or at automated fee machines throughout the park. Payment can be made with cash or a credit card and the admission fee is good for seven days. Tape your receipt to your windshield or display your national park pass on your hangtag. Campgrounds will also check for valid passes and give you a permit to attach to your window.

The National Park Service also offers free admission on several days throughout the year, including Martin Luther King, Jr. Day, National Public Lands Day, Veterans Day and the first day of National Park Week. It's best to arrive early on these days, as the park is usually quite crowded.

Park Passes

A number of discount park passes are also available at all national park visitor centers. See if you qualify for one, as it may help trim your travel budget.

Access Pass

This free lifetime pass provides for free admission to all national parks, and is available to U.S. citizens or residents with a permanent disability. Applicants must provide documentation of a permanent disability, and prove residency or citizenship. The pass also offers a 50% discount on campsites and boat launch fees. It generally does not provide for a discount on fees charged by concessionaires.

Military Pass

The free annual Military Pass provides for free park admission, and is available to active members of the Army, Navy, Air Force, Marines and Coast Guard. Reserve and National Guard Members are also eligible. A Common Access Card or Military ID (Form 1173) is required to obtain this pass.

Senior Pass

This lifetime pass provides free park admission, and is available to U.S. citizens or permanent residents age 62 or older. The cost of the pass is $80. An annual Senior Pass is also available for $20, and the cost for this annual pass can be applied to the purchase of a lifetime pass. Proof of age and residency or citizenship are required. The pass also offers a 50% discount on campsites and boat launch fees. It generally does not provide for a discount on fees charged by concessionaires.

Annual Pass

If you plan on visiting a number of national parks throughout the year, the Annual Pass may be a good deal for you. This non-transferable pass costs $80 and it's good for free park admission to all national parks for the entire year. It's an especially attractive deal if you live near a national park, or are planning a road trip that includes a number of national parks. You can also order this pass by calling (888) 275-8747.

Annual 4th Grade Pass

This free annual pass is available to all 4th graders and is valid for the duration of the 4th grade school year and the following summer. Paper vouchers can be obtained at www.everykidinapark.gov and exchanged for an Annual 4th Grade Pass at any national park entrance. This pass is also available to home-schooled students.

Death Valley National Park Annual Pass

If you're planning several trips to Death Valley within a year, the Death Valley National Park Annual Pass could save you a few bucks. It costs $55 and it's valid for 12 months from the date of purchase. It's good for unlimited visits to Death Valley National Park for the purchaser and others in the vehicle.

Information

Although there is a variety of contact information listed at the end of the Death Valley chapter, the social media contacts are particularly important. In my experience — and that of my readers — the parks are quite responsive to inquiries received via social media; so if you have a time sensitive question I recommend either posting it on their Twitter or Facebook feed, or using Facebook to send a private message to them.

ɔrized Park Concessionaires

e lodgings inside Death Valley National Park are operated by
auth͟c͟ zed concessionaires, who have contracted with the National Park
Service, and operate under strict guidelines. They are responsible for the
daily operations of the facilities, as well as improvements and upgrades.
It's important to deal with these concessionaires directly when you make a
reservation; as not only will you get the best price there, but you will also
have access to employees that can block the accessible rooms and describe
the access details of each available unit. Unfortunately these concessionaires
do not always come up first in internet searches because paid advertisements
appear before them. Some of these paid advertisements even list "national
park lodges" that are located many miles outside the parks, which is very
misleading to people who are unfamiliar with the geography of the parks. The
authorized concessionaires in Death Valley National Park are listed below.
Again, deal directly with these concessionaires for all lodging reservations.

Death Valley National Park Concessionaires

Xanterra Travel Collection
(800) 236-7916
www.oasisatdeathvalley.com
www.facebook.com/oasisatdeathvalley
The Inn at Death Valley
The Ranch at Death Valley

Ortega National Parks
(760) 786-7090
www.deathvalleyhotels.com
Stovepipe Wells Village Hotel

What is an Accessible Guestroom?

There are a wide variety of accessible guestrooms included in this book.
Some will work for wheelchair-users, while others are a better choice
for slow walkers. It's important to note that access regulations can vary
depending on the age, size and sometimes even the location of the property.
So in the end there's not one single definition of an accessible guestroom
that will work for everyone.

An accessible guestroom can have a bathroom with a roll-in shower, a
transfer-type shower or a tub/shower combination. Some larger properties

may have rooms with each configuration; while properties with less than 50 rooms will most likely only have accessible rooms with a tub/shower combination.

Toilets are another matter entirely. The regulations specify that a toilet in an accessible guestroom must be 17–19 inches high. Admittedly that height won't work for everyone, so if you need a higher toilet just ask for a toilet riser.

Bed height is a bit harder to fix. Since beds are considered removable, they are not covered in the access regulations, and to be honest there's a wide range of bed heights out there. That's why bed heights are noted in this book. Most wheelchair-users prefer lower beds, while people with knee or hip issues or have problems standing and bending generally like higher beds. Some people who prefer higher beds travel with furniture risers, or ask the hotel if they have some wood blocks to raise the bed. Lowering a bed is more difficult. If it's not a platform bed it can sometimes be taken off the frame, but some platform beds just can't be lowered. Sometimes it's also possible to put a lower rollaway bed in the room. If after reading the access descriptions in this book, you feel that bed height might be a problem, contact the property directly to see if they are able to work with you.

The bottom line is, there's not one standard definition of an accessible guestroom. With that in mind, this book contains detailed access descriptions and photographs to help readers pick rooms that best suit their needs. And while one room might not work for you personally, keep in mind that it may be the perfect fit for another reader.

What is an Accessible Trail?

This book contains a number of trails that are rated as accessible by the National Park Service. It's important to understand that a trail does not have to be flat and paved in order to be accessible. The accessibility rules are laid out in the Architectural Barriers Act Accessibility Guidelines for Outdoor Developed Areas, that were published in the Federal Register on September 26, 2013. This rule became effective on November 25, 2013, for newly developed and substantially altered trails in federal outdoor developed areas.

This section is included to explain what you can expect to find on a trail that is rated as accessible in a federal area. It does not necessarily mean that you can access it, but rather that it follows the standards and regulations for an accessible trail. For this reason, even if a trail is rated as accessible, the access features of it will still be described in this book. Additionally, many trails that are not rated as accessible are included in this book, as they will work for many wheelchair-users and slow walkers.

Surface and Width

- Accessible trails must be firm and stable
- There can be no openings, gaps or tread obstacles along an accessible trail
- Accessible trails must be at least 36-inches wide

Running Slope

- No more than 30% of the the total length of an accessible trail may have a running slope greater than 1:12 (8.33%). A 1:12 slope includes a one-foot rise ever 12 feet
- Running slopes between 1:12 (8.33%) and 1:10 (10%) are allowed in 30-foot segments, with resting intervals at the top and bottom of each segment
- The running slope of an accessible trail may never exceed 1:8 (12%)

Service Animals in National Parks

In October 2018, the National Park Service (NPS) issued a new system-wide policy regarding the use of service animals by persons with disabilities in national parks. The revised policy aligns the NPS policy with the standards established by the Department of Justice (DOJ) and the Americans with Disabilities Act (ADA).

Under the policy, a service animal is defined as any dog that is individually trained to do work or perform tasks for the benefit of an individual with a disability, including a physical, sensory, psychiatric, intellectual, or other mental disability.

Service animals-in-training are not considered service animals.

Although the DOJ definition of a service animal only refers to a dog, the NPS must make reasonable modifications to policies, practices, or procedures to permit the use of a miniature horse by a person with a disability if the miniature horse has been individually trained to do work or perform tasks for the benefit of the individual with a disability.

The work or tasks performed by a service animal must be directly related to the individual's disability. Some examples of work or tasks performed may include:

- Assist individuals who are blind with navigation
- Alert individuals who are deaf to the presence of people or sounds
- Pull a wheelchair
- Alert individuals to the presence of allergens or the onset of a seizure
- Retrieve items
- Provide physical support and assistance to individuals with mobility disabilities
- Help individuals manage psychiatric and neurological disabilities

The crime deterrent effects of an animal's presence and the provision of emotional support, well-being, comfort, or companionship do not constitute work or tasks for the purposes of this definition.

Emotional support animals, therapy animals and companion animals are not recognized as service animals by the NPS.

All animals that are not classified as service animals are considered pets, and are subject to the pet regulations of the parks, which can be found on the individual park websites. Service animals are allowed access to all areas of the park, including lodgings, restaurants, trails and attractions.

It should also be noted that although some organizations sell "service animal registration" documents on-line, these documents do not convey any rights under the ADA; and the DOJ and the NPS does not recognize them as proof that a dog is a service animal.

For more information on the ADA (and the NPS) definition of a service animal, visit www.ada.gov.

Death Valley National Park

Death Valley as seen from Dantes View

Known as Tümpisa by the Timbisha Shoshone Indians who settled there, Death Valley was given its English moniker by a group of 49ers who were heading to the California gold rush. Although only one person in the ill fated party died, it was a genuine struggle for the survivors to find food and water as they traversed the barren desert. When they finally made their way out, one man turned around and muttered, "Goodbye, Death Valley," and somehow the name stuck.

The hottest, driest and lowest point in North America, Death Valley is the largest national park in the lower 48 states. And with over three million acres of wilderness area, there's a huge diversity in the flora and fauna throughout the park. From majestic sand dunes and salt flats, to snow capped peaks, a lush oasis and even a massive crater, there's something for just about everyone at this remote national treasure. And even though the name is a bit foreboding, thanks to access upgrades over the years, Death Valley is a good choice for wheelchair-users and slow walkers.

There are no entrance stations at Death Valley National Park — visitors pay their entrance fees at automated kiosks or at the visitor center — however there are several roads that lead to the national park.

On the west side of the park Highway 178 connects to Highway 190, which enters the park just east of Panamint Springs. This West Entrance is about 70 miles northeast of Ridgecrest. Alternatively, Highway 190 begins in Olancha and travels 40 miles east to another West Entrance. This entrance is located 50 miles southeast of Lone Pine, and can be accessed by Highway 136 which connects to Highway 190.

On the south side of the park, Highway 127 runs from Interstate 15 to the Shoshone Entrance, which is about 85 miles north of Baker.

Over on the east side of the park. Highway 374 runs from Highway 95 to the Northeast Entrance, about 13 miles southwest of Beatty. Highway 95 also connects to Highway 373 in Lathrop Wells. The road transitions to Highway 127 when it enters California, connects with Highway 190 at Death Valley Junction, and continues on to the East Entrance. This route is about 33 miles long. Alternatively, Highway 267 leads from Scotty's Junction at Highway 95 and travels 26 miles southwest to the Scotty's Castle Entrance.

The Basics

Road Conditions and Operating Seasons

Death Valley National Park is open year-round, however some roads can be temporarily closed due to weather conditions. Dantes View Road and Upper Wildrose Road can close in the winter due to snow and ice. Badwater Road, portions of Highway 190 and Scotty's Castle Road into Grapevine Canyon are subject to flooding and can close after heavy rains. The official park website is usually updated when new closures occur. The Death Valley Road Conditions Facebook Page (www.facebook.com/DeathValleyRoadConditions) is also a good source for updated road conditions

For more information on current road conditions, call (760) 786-3200.

The fall and winter are pleasant seasons to visit Death Valley. The daytime temperatures are mild in the lower elevations, and the evenings can get chilly. Some ice can also form on the roads at the higher elevations during the winter.

The spring wildflower blooms are lovely in the desert; however the timing can be tricky. The blooms usually burst forth a few weeks after a heavy rain; however the rains can also cause flooding and road closures.

Summer is the least hospitable time in Death Valley; in fact the park holds the world record for the highest air temperature — 134 degrees at Furnace Creek on July 10, 1913. Summer temperatures routinely top 120 degrees, with nighttime lows in the mid-90s. Still some folks consider it a personal challenge to visit at this time.

Weather updates are available on the park's Facebook page and Twitter feed.

Altitude

The highest point in Death Valley National Park is Telescope Peak, with an elevation of 11,043 feet. That said the highest place navigable by vehicle are the Charcoal Kilns on Emigrant Canyon Road, at an elevation of 6,800 feet. The good news is, that a good chunk of Death Valley is located below sea level; in fact Badwater Basin is the lowest point in North America, at 282 feet below sea level.

Badwater Basin — the lowest point in North America

Although the symptoms of altitude sickness generally do not appear at elevations under 8,000 feet, wheelchair-users, slow walkers and people with compromised immune systems may feel the effects of increased altitudes at significantly lower elevations. Symptoms can include headaches, dizziness, shortness of breath, lethargy, insomnia and gastrointestinal disturbances. If you are unfamiliar with the effects that higher elevations have on your body, it's best to take it slow and drink plenty of water for the first few days at any increased elevation, especially if you live at sea level. Additionally, you may want to consult your doctor regarding the effects that increased elevations may have on your specific condition. To assist you in your travel planning, elevations are noted at the beginning of each section.

Airport

The closest commercial airport to Death Valley is McCarran International Airport in Las Vegas. It's about a two-hour drive via Highway 95 through Death Valley Junction. Accessible van rentals are available at Mobility Works (www.mobilityworks.com, 877-275-4915), the Ability Center (www.abilitycenter.com, 702-434-3030), and Wheelers Van Rentals (wheelersvanrentals.com, 866-859-8880) in Las Vegas.

The second closest commercial airport is Los Angeles International Airport. It's located about four hours away via Interstate 15 and Baker. Accessible van rentals are available at Mobility Works (www.mobilityworks.com, 877-275-4915), Accessible Vans of America - Wheelchair Getaways (www.accessiblevans.com, 650-589-5554) and the Ability Center (www.abilitycenter.com, 562-634-5962) in the Los Angeles area.

Amtrak

The Southwest Chief, which runs from Chicago to Los Angeles, stops at Barstow, which is about a 2.5-hour drive from the park. There are no accessible van rental outlets in Barstow, but several national rental car companies have offices there. Alternatively you can take the train to Los Angeles and rent an accessible van there, or see if one of the Los Angeles companies (see list under "Airports") will deliver an accessible rental van to Barstow. It's a four-hour drive from Los Angeles to the park.

Connectivity

Cell phone service is extremely limited in the park, and signal strength varies by location, but there's usually a decent signal at the park lodgings. Free Wi-Fi is available in the Stovepipe Wells Village Hotel business center, which is located next to the gift shop. It is also available to guests at The Inn at Death Valley and the Ranch at Death Valley. There is no public Wi-Fi at the visitor center or any other National Park Service (NPS) locations.

Wheelchairs

Wheelchairs are available for loan on a first-come basis at the Furnace Creek Visitor Center.

Ranger Programs

Free ranger-led programs are presented at several locations throughout the park, from mid-November through April. A schedule of the programs is available at the Furnace Creek Visitor Center. Access details on the program venues are contained in this book.

Camping

Death Valley has both NPS operated campgrounds as well as privately operated campgrounds. The only reservable NPS campground is Furnace Creek Campground. Although the campground is open all year, reservations are only accepted for the peak season, from October through April. Reservations can be made up to six months in advance at www.recreation.gov or (877) 444-6777. During the rest of the year campsites are only available on a walk-in basis.

Campsites at the rest of the NPS campgrounds are only available on a walk-in basis.

Panamint Springs Campground is operated by Panamint Springs Resort (www.panamintsprings.com). Reservations can be made year-round by calling (775) 482-7680 or e-mailing reservations@panamintsprings.com.

Stovepipe Wells RV park is operated by Ortega National Parks. Reservations can be made year-round at www.deathvalleyhotels.com or by calling (760) 786-7090.

Fiddlers' Campground is operated by the Xanterra Travel Collection. Reservations can be made year-round at www.oasisatdeathvalley.com or by calling (760) 786-2345

Pets

There are some restrictions on pets in Death Valley. They are not allowed inside most buildings or on trails. They are permitted on park roads and at campgrounds and picnic areas, but they must always be kept on a maximum six-foot long leash, and never left unattended. There are no restrictions on service animals, but they must meet the legal definition outlined in the first chapter of this book.

Furnace Creek - Badwater

Elevation – 282 Feet Below Sea Level to 5,475 Feet

Located in the southeast area of the park near the intersection of Highway 190 and Badwater Road, Furnace Creek was once the base of operations for the Pacific Coast Borax Company. Today it's the park's major hub, and home to the visitor center, park headquarters, two lodges and a good collection of visitor services. Combined with Badwater Basin, the bulk of the area is located below sea level; with the notable exception of Dantes View, which towers over the desert and offers an impressive overlook of the vast expanse.

Attractions

Furnace Creek Visitor Center

Located next to Furnace Creek Campground, this visitor center features accessible parking near the entrance with barrier-free access to the building. Inside there's plenty of room to maneuver a wheelchair through the bookstore and over to the auditorium, and there's accessible seating next to

Furnace Creek Visitor Center

companion seats in the auditorium. There's also a ranger information de where you can get additional information, pay entrance fees and get park maps.

There's good access through the interpretive exhibits which give visitors a good overview of the park. The exhibits focus on the weather, night sky, native people and the flora and fauna of Death Valley. There are also a number of interactive exhibits and a short film about the park at the visitor center.

Accessible restrooms are located outside. There is also a small picnic area but the tables are located on cement platforms that are about four-inches high. Additionally, there's level access from the visitor center to the Furnace Creek Campground amphitheater, where evening programs are held.

Borax Museum

The outdoor Borax Museum is located behind the Trading Post at the Ranch at Death Valley. Accessible parking is located in the lot next door, with level access over to the museum. There's ramp access down to the exhibits from the back porch of the Trading Post, and plenty of room to maneuver a wheelchair around the old mining and railroad equipment. There is also barrier-free access to the museum via the sidewalk on the left side of the Trading Post. Printed guides about the exhibits are located in the box next to the front door of the Trading Post. Highlights include a hand operated stamp mill, a railroad crew car, several stagecoaches, a handmade ore car and even a Conestoga wagon. And don't miss Old Dinah, the 1894 steam tractor that replaced the 20 mule teams that originally hauled borax out of the canyon. It was found abandoned by the Keane Wonder Mine. Best of all, there's no admission charge to the museum.

Zabriskie Point

This popular viewpoint, which is located on Highway 190 just east of the Inn at Death Valley, was originally constructed by the Pacific Coast Borax Company back in the 1920s. Named for the company's founder, Christian Zabriskie, it offers a panoramic view of the Death Valley badlands. There's accessible parking next to the accessible vault toilets, and level access over to the paved path to the overlook. That said the paved pathway to the overlook is extremely steep and not doable for manual wheelchairs. I did however see a few scooters and a number of slow walkers manage the climb though. There are benches to stop and rest along the way, and even if you can't make it to the top of the 100-yard trail, there are still some good

The paved path to Zabriskie Point

views along the way. At the top there are several interpretive panels, and a commanding view of the badlands with the salt flats in the distance.

Dantes View

Named for the tale of Dante's trip through purgatory — because there are numerous references to the dark underworld found in other Death Valley attraction names — this popular viewpoint is located off of Highway 190, east of 20 Mule Team Canyon. Vehicles over 25 feet are prohibited on the 13-mile drive to the overlook, and the last mile has a steep 15 percent grade. That said the overlook offers one of the best views of the valley and it has good wheelchair access, so it's definitely worth the drive.

There's accessible parking at the top, with curb-cut access over to the viewpoint. A level sidewalk leads around the overlook, and since it's located on the spine of the Black Mountains it offers an excellent view of Death Valley Basin. To the west you'll see Badwater Basin, the Panamint Range and Telescope Peak, and to the east there's a good view of the Greenwater Range. For obvious reasons, this viewpoint is a favorite for photographers. The windshield views on the drive to and from the viewpoint are also excellent.

Harmony Borax Works

These remains of the Harmony Borax Works are located west of the visitor center, off of Highway 190. There's accessible parking in the small lot, with barrier-free access to an asphalt trail that winds around the ruins of this borax refinery, which operated in the 1880s. There's a slight uphill grade on the first part of the trail, but make sure and take the loop in a counter-clockwise direction for the best access. It's a .20-mile walk to the lower exhibits, which include a 20 mule team wagon which was used to haul borax out of Death Valley. There are also the remains of the refinery and some processing equipment across the trail from the wagon. From there, the trail continues uphill and loops around to the other side of the refinery, and offers a closer look at the equipment. Some manual wheelchair-users may require assistance because of the grade; however even if you can't manage the whole trail, the trek out to the lower exhibit is worth the walk. All in all it's a half-mile loop, and although there are a few parts of the asphalt that are in need of repair, they are easy to dodge. An essential stop on any Death Valley itinerary.

Devils Golf Course

These delicate salt formations are located a half-mile off of Badwater Road, just south of Artists Drive. The dirt road that leads out to the viewpoint is

Harmony Borax Works

graded and passable in a low clearance vehicle. There's no striped parking at the viewpoint, but there's plenty of room to parallel park an adapted van there. This area of rock salt has been so eroded by the wind and rain, that jagged spires protrude up through the deposits; and in keeping with the underworld references in the park, it's been said that only the devil could play golf on this rugged course. And if you listen closely you can hear the pops and cracks of the salt crystals as they burst apart and expand and contract in the heat.

Badwater

The lowest point in North America, Badwater is located just south of the Devils Golf Course, off of Badwater Road. There's accessible parking near the accessible vault toilets, with curb-cut access up to the sidewalk .And although the parking lot often fills to capacity, there always seems to be at least one accessible parking spot available. From the parking area there's ramp access to a short boardwalk that leads out to the salt flats. There's also level access over to the Badwater sign — a popular photo spot — which touts the elevation of 282 feet below sea level.

There's a well trod level path out across the salt flats, as a result of years of foot traffic. The entire trail is a little over a mile long, but as you get farther out it gets bumpier, due to less traffic. The first quarter-mile is pretty tramped down and doable for most wheelchair-users and slow walkers. Be sure and bring plenty of water and wear a hat, as the sun is pretty intense in this area. Additionally, during heavy rains the basin becomes a lake, and although it's not passable at that time, it makes for a great photo stop. Don't forget to look up to get a gander at Dantes View, the popular overlook that's precariously perched some 5,000 feet above the salt flats.

Mormon Point

Located south of Badwater, between mile markers 32 and 33, this historic point is marked by a small NPS sign. There's no official parking, but there's room enough on the side of the road to pull over and parallel park an adapted van. This point is actually a large promontory of the Black Mountain Range, composed of ash beds, mudstone and rocks. The view of the Panamints is also nice from this vantage point. It's unclear how this geological feature got it's name, but some early references indicate that the Mormons did travel through Death Valley.

View from Mormon Point

Ashford Mill

What's left of the historic Ashford Mill is located south of Mormon Point off of Badwater Road. There's a graded dirt road that leads out to an interpretive plaque, and plenty of room to parallel park an adapted van in the level unpaved parking area. The Ashford Brothers once owned this mill, where the ore from the Golden Treasure mine was processed for shipment to the smelter. There's no wheelchair access down to the ruins, but you can get a good view of what's left from the overlook. There are also a couple of picnic tables in an unshaded dirt area, and an accessible vault toilet located nearby. It's worth a stop for the desert view, and since most folks don't get south of Badwater, you'll probably have the site to yourself.

Trails

Bicycle Path to Harmony Borax Works

The 1.5-mile bicycle path that leads from the visitor center to Harmony Borax Works is a good choice for wheelchair-users and slow walkers. The level trail runs parallel to the highway, and offers some nice desert views. It's a good choice for folks who want a longer jaunt, or for photographers who want to stop for photos along the way.

Picnic Areas

Furnace Creek Picnic Area

Located next to the gas station on Highway 190, this small picnic area offers some welcome respite from the desert sun. There's no formal parking lot, but there's plenty of room to parallel park an adapted van in the dirt parking area near the tables. There's level access over to the shaded tables, which have room for a wheelchair at the ends. It's a pretty basic picnic area, with no restroom facilities, but it offers a nice view of the surrounding hills.

Scenic Drives   ~ 30 minutes

20 Mule Team Canyon

Most folks zip on by this scenic drive off of Highway 190, on their way to visit the more popular Dantes View. This 2.5-mile drive winds up and down through the colorful eroded badlands, and offers an off-the-beaten-track experience without having to trek through the desert for days. This one-way dirt road is graded, and suitable for even low clearance vehicles. That said, it closes during heavy rains as it's subject to flooding. Interestingly enough this narrow road was never traversed by the infamous 20 mule teams, as it wasn't wide enough to accommodate them. There aren't really any places to stop and park along the drive, but the windshield views are excellent. And if there aren't any cars behind you, you can always roll down the window and snap a few photos. Although the drive is pretty short the road winds up and down through the badlands, so it takes about 30 minutes to complete. It's a great stop after Zabriskie Point, on the way to Dantes View.

20 Mule Team Drive

Artists Drive ✗   *9 miles - ∼ 30 minutes*

Located off Badwater Road just north of the Devils Golf Course, this one-way drive winds up and through the colorful mountains and offers an up-close-and-personal view of this scenic Death Valley landscape. There are a few wide spots to stop along the way, but for the most part it's a colorful windshield view. The posted speed limit is 25 mph, but most folks go much slower so they can take in all the beauty. And as the light changes so does the view. Up on top, there's also a good view of the salt flats in the distance. One of the highlights of the drive is Artists Palette overlook, which is located off the main road. There's accessible parking next to the accessible vault toilet, and a barrier-free path over to the interpretive plaque. The volcanic minerals in the hills, which have been chemically altered by the extreme heat, cause the vibrant hillside colors. It is indeed a colorful palette. Although the drive is only nine miles long, allow at least a half-hour for photo stops along the way. And since vehicles over 25 feet long are prohibited, you won't encounter any tour buses on this scenic drive.

Lodging

Ranch at Death Valley

Death Valley National Park, CA 92328
(800) 236-7916
www.oasisatdeathvalley.com

Originally a working ranch, the Ranch at Death Valley welcomed its first guests in 1933. A family-friendly favorite for years, the property received a major facelift in 2018, with a $100 million renovation project. Not only did this massive undertaking modernize the facilities, but it also added new amenities to the property. Today two new Spanish Colonial Revival buildings grace the entrance, and house the registration area, new restaurants and a well-stocked store. Add in some lush new landscaping, and you have a totally revitalized property.

Accessible parking is available in front of the new registration building, which is located right off Highway 190. There's barrier-free access to the front door, and good pathway access over to the registration desk. The new town square park — a relaxing green space with accessible pathways and benches — borders the registration building on the hotel side of the building.

Town Square Park at the Ranch at Death Valley

Room 402 at the Ranch at Death Valley (view 1)

The Ranch at Death Valley has four accessible rooms with roll-in showers and four accessible rooms with tub/shower combinations. Room 402, which is a deluxe accessible room, is located a short walk from the office, near the swimming pool and sports courts. Accessible parking is located near the room, with barrier-free access to the front door.

Room 402 at the Ranch at Death Valley (view 2)

Access features include wide doorways, lever handles, low-pile carpet and good pathway access. The room is furnished with a 25-inch high full bed and a 25-inch high twin bed, with an access aisle between them. Other furnishings include a desk with a chair, a chest of drawers, an easy chair and a refrigerator. There's also a sliding glass door that leads out to a shared patio, and offers a refreshing view of the verdant lawn, with the mountains in the distance. There's plenty of room for a wheelchair on the patio, which features level access from inside.

The bathroom boasts a full five-foot turning radius and is equipped with a roll-in shower with grab bars, a hand-held showerhead and a built-in corner shower seat. The toilet grab bars are located on the back and right walls (as seated), and the bathroom also includes a roll-under sink.

The property is spread out, but accessible pathways lead to and from the rooms and all of the facilities. There's good access to the public areas of the hotel, including the restaurants, General Store, Trading Post and golf course. There's ramp access to the pool area, and barrier-free access to the lift-equipped pool, showers and changing rooms. There are also two accessible picnic tables located in the level picnic area adjacent to the bus parking area. All in all, the Ranch at Death Valley is a very comfortable and accessible property.

The Ranch at Death Valley is open year-round.

Bathroom in room 402 at the Ranch at Death Valley

Inn at Death Valley

Highway 190
Death Valley National Park, CA 92328
(800) 236-7916
www.oasisatdeathvalley.com

Nestled into the mountainside, the historic Inn at Death Valley offers a commanding desert view framed by the towering Panamint Mountains. This property received a major renovation in 2018, when it was completely gutted and redone from top to bottom. The result is a modern AAA Four Diamond Inn that exudes an aura of casual elegance. It combines the best of both worlds — the rugged old west and the modern 21st century. And with more green space, less cement and a new grove of date palms, it's a verdant, relaxing and luxurious place to spend a few nights.

Although steps grace the front entrance of this 1927 property, there's elevator access up to the lobby on the side of the building, just around the corner from the valet stand. There's also accessible parking behind the building, with level access through the tunnel to an elevator.

There's barrier-free access throughout the third-floor lobby, and excellent views of the surrounding desert from just about anywhere on this floor. Accessible restrooms are located near the registration desk, and there's good pathway access to the historic lobby library, which is filled with comfortable furniture.

The Inn at Death Valley has accessible rooms, casitas, and a suite. Room 323, which is located on the lobby level, features wide doorways, lever handles, low-pile carpet and good pathway access. It's furnished with a 23-inch high king-sized bed with wheelchair access on both sides. Other furnishings include a desk with a chair, two night stands, a refrigerator, and an easy chair.

The bathroom features a full five-foot turning radius and is equipped with a roll-in shower with grab bars, a hand-held showerhead and a fold-down shower bench. Other access features include a toilet with grab bars on the back and left walls (as seated), and a roll-under sink. Top it off with a lowered robe hook, and you have a very accessible room.

The new casitas are located a short drive away from the main lobby; however casita guests are issued their own golf carts at check-in. If a guest is unable to drive a golf cart, valet service to and from the casita is available.

Room 323 at the Inn at Death Valley

Bathroom in room 323 at the Inn at Death Valley

Casita 501 is an accessible casita. Access features include wide doorways, lever handles and excellent pathway access. The casita includes a living area that's furnished with a 13-inch high sleeper sofa, a desk with a chair, an easy chair and a chest of drawers. Around the corner there's a wet bar with a refrigerator and a microwave. There's also level access out to the spacious patio which borders an expansive lawn area. The patio includes a table with chairs, but there's still plenty of room for a wheelchair.

Casita 501 at the Inn at Death Valley

The bedroom is furnished with two 22-inch high queen-sized beds with an access aisle between them, a chest of drawers and a night stand. The spacious bathroom is equipped with a roll-in shower with grab bars, a hand-held showerhead and a fold-down shower bench located close to the

Bedroom in Casita 501 at the Inn at Death Valley

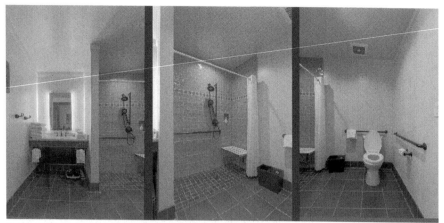

Bathroom in Casita 501 at the Inn at Death Valley

shower controls. The toilet grab bars are located on the back and left walls (as seated) and the bathroom also includes a roll-under sink.

This casita adjoins another accessible casita that has the same basic access features, but it's furnished with a king-sized bed. The accessible casitas are located near the lift-equipped swimming pool; however there's also an accessible parking place in front of the pool if you'd prefer to drive. These new casitas at the Inn at Death Valley are the most accessible and luxurious accommodations in the park.

Living space in Casita 501 at the Inn at Death Valley

There's good wheelchair access to the public areas of the inn, including the restaurant, bar and the new library. Even if you don't stay at the property, stop in for a bite to eat or a drink, and enjoy the expansive view of the lush grounds, towering palms and the desert in the distance.

Although the Inn at Death Valley is usually open year-round, due to Covid-19 it will be closed until October 1, 2020.

Fiddlers' Campground

Operated by the Xanterra Travel Collection this campground is located near the Furnace Creek gas station off of Highway 190.There are no designated accessible campsites but the area is fairly level so most of the sites are doable for wheelchair-users and slow walkers. The surface is covered in gravel, and accessible restrooms are located behind the last row, across the street from the golf course. Guests also receive a shower and pool pass to the Ranch at Death Valley. There are communal grills at this campground, and each campsite has a picnic table. There are no hook-ups at this campground.

Fiddlers' Campground is open year-round, and reservations can be made by calling (760) 786-2345 or online at www.oasisatdeathvalley.com.

Fiddlers' Campground

Furnace Creek Campground

Located next to the Furnace Creek Visitor Center, this campground has eight wheelchair-accessible campsites. All of the accessible campsites are located near an accessible restroom or vault toilet, and water. They each have a paved parking space, a raised grill and an accessible picnic table. The accessible walk-in tent sites also have accessible parking in front of them.

Sites 49, 74 and 77 are accessible electric campsites, sites 22 and 84 are accessible non-electric campsites and sites 115, 147 and 149 are accessible walk-in campsites.

There is also level access to the campground amphitheater, which is located between site 77 and the visitor center. Seating is on benches without backs, and there's plenty of room to park a wheelchair or scooter in front or on the sides.

Furnace Creek Campground is open year-round; however reservations are only accepted during the peak season, from October through March. Reservations can be made up to six months in advance at www.recreation.gov or (877) 444-6777. During the rest of the year campsites are available on a walk-in basis.

Furnace Creek Campground

Sunset Campground

The largest campground in the park, Sunset Campground, is located off of Highway 190 on Texas Springs Road. It's a pretty basic campground, but the views of the surrounding badlands are impressive.

There are 16 accessible campsites in back of the accessible restroom that's equipped with large stalls and roll-under sinks. The sites are all level and paved, and although the entire campground is flat, the standard campsites are covered in gravel. There are no hook-ups or picnic tables at this campground.

Sunset Campground is open from mid-October to mid-April. All sites are available on a walk-in basis.

Sunset Campground

Texas Springs Campground

Located just down the road from Sunset Campground, Texas Springs Campground boasts equally impressive badlands views. Accessible campsites 59, 60 and 61 are level, and each one has a raised grill and an accessible picnic table. They are located close to accessible restrooms which have large stalls and roll-under sinks. There are no hook-ups at this campground, and generators are prohibited.

Texas Springs Campground is open from mid-October to mid-May. All sites are available on a walk-in basis.

Texas Springs Campground

Dining

1849 Buffet ← 2½ ★

Located in the restaurant building at the Ranch at Death Valley, the 1849
Buffet features good pathway access and plenty of room to maneuver a
wheelchair around the tables. There's wheelchair access to the building
via a ramp up to the General Store on the north side of the building. This
buffet restaurant features breakfast favorites in the morning, a salad bar and
sandwich makings at lunch, and some American and international entrees
during the dinner hour.

Last Kind Words Saloon & Steakhouse 4 ★

There's level access to this western themed steakhouse from the adjacent
1849 Buffet, and plenty of room to maneuver a wheelchair inside. There is
also an accessible entrance on the south side of the building, across from
the registration building. Open for lunch and dinner, the menu includes
a nice selection of sandwiches, snacks and small plates during the day,
and steaks, chops, fish and other favorites in the evening. A full bar is also
available.

Date Grove Coffee & Ice Cream

Tucked away between the General Store and the 1849 Buffet, this small
counter offers hot dogs, chili, pizza, coffee drinks, milkshakes and ice
cream. There's level access to the counter with plenty of room to maneuver
a wheelchair. It's a good place to pick up a quick snack or to enjoy an ice
cream treat.

19th Hole

Located next to the pro shop at the Furnace Creek Golf Course at Death
Valley, the 19th Hole is open in the afternoons. There's accessible parking
near the pro shop, across the street from Fiddlers' Campground, and level
access to this small bar and grill. There is also a short level path to the 19th
Hole from the parking lot across the street from the Trading Post. The
menu includes burgers, sandwiches, hot dogs, beer and wine. There's also a
nice view of the golf course from the patio tables.

Inn Dining Room

[handwritten: bfast + dinner 3½-4 ☆ $74 steak crazy prices]

Located just off the main lobby of The Inn at Death Valley, this fine dining restaurant is open for breakfast, lunch and dinner. There's level access to the restaurant, which also offers patio dining when the weather permits. This restaurant serves breakfast favorites in the morning, a selection of salads, sandwiches and soups for lunch, and a creative menu of beef, chicken, fish, pasta and vegetarian offerings in the evening. The dress code for dinner is resort attire, which translates to no t-shirts or tank tops. Advance reservations, which are highly recommended, and are available to inn guests.

[handwritten: no lunch now?]

Inn Lobby Lounge

[handwritten: only 4 items on menu]

Located next to the dining room, the lounge is open for lunch and dinner, and offers drinks and small plates. There's level access to the lounge from the lobby and the dining room, and you just can't beat the commanding view of the desert landscape.

Inn Pool Bar

There's level access to this poolside bar which is open in the afternoons. Accessible parking is located near the pool, and it's just a short accessible walk away from the casitas.

Timbisha Village Tacos

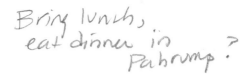

Timbisha Village Tacos

Located on Timbisha Shoshone land, this small taco shop is just east of the Ranch at Death Valley, off of Highway 190. You can't miss it, as the turn is well marked with signs. There's no accessible parking in the paved lot, but it is level. Unfortunately there's about a three-inch step up to the accessible front walk, due to erosion, but there's barrier-free access to the front door. It's a pretty basic restaurant that offers Indian tacos, burritos, taco salad, and shaved ice. There's ample room to maneuver a wheelchair up to the counter, and there's a roomy accessible restroom in the rear. The food is good, but be prepared to wait as it's usually only staffed with a few employees. And although the hours vary, this restaurant is usually open for lunch. To-go food is also available.

Services

General Store

The large building, which is located kitty corner from the Trading Post at the Ranch at Death Valley, houses the general store as well as some other public facilities. There's accessible parking in the large lot in front, with ramp access up to the front porch. There's level access to the store and plenty of room to maneuver a wheelchair inside. Offerings include beer, wine, cold drinks, frozen entrees, books, souvenirs and gifts. There are also accessible restrooms located to the right of the inside entrance.

Trading Post

Located kitty corner from the restaurant building at the Ranch at Death Valley, this small store offers souvenirs, soft drinks, snacks and books. There's ramp access to the front door and level access out to the back porch which overlooks the outdoor Borax Museum. The Trading Post is usually open on the weekends.

Gas Station

Located on Highway 190, next to the Ranch at Death Valley, this small gas station is open 24 hours for credit and debit card purchases. There is also level access over to the cashier window, which is manned during the day. The bathrooms, which are located on the left side of the building, are not wheelchair-accessible. There is also a dump station located across the street from the gas station.

Laundry

A coin operated guest laundry is located at the Ranch at Death Valley, behind the picnic area. There is one step up to the building, and room to maneuver a wheelchair around the machines inside.

Showers

Daily shower and pool passes to the facilities at the Ranch at Death Valley are available for $10 at the Ranch at Death Valley registration desk. These passes are available to the general public and they include unlimited access to the pool and showers for the whole day. Visitors who purchase the passes are issued gate keys so they can come and go as they please. The pool includes a wheelchair lift, and each side of the shower house features an accessible stall and roll-in showers that have grab bars, a hand-held showerhead and a portable shower bench.

Post Office

The post office is located kitty corner from the Trading Post, and across the street from the town square park. There's accessible parking in front with level access to the building.

Furnace Creek Golf Course at Death Valley

Located at the Ranch at Death Valley, the Furnace Creek Golf Course at Death Valley is the lowest golf course in the world, with an elevation of 214 feet below sea level. Accessible parking is located near the pro shop across from Fiddlers' Campground, with level access to the pro shop and the 19th Hole bar and grill. There is also a short level path to the golf course from the parking lot across the street from the Trading Post. Accessible restrooms are located across from the accessible parking space at Fiddlers' Campground. Even if you don't golf, it's a beautiful course to visit.

Stovepipe Wells - Emigrant Canyon

Elevation – 10 Feet to 6,800 Feet

L ocated northwest of Furnace Creek, Stovepipe Wells takes its name from a historic well nearby that was marked with a stovepipe, so thirsty travelers could easily locate the much needed water. The area is just above sea level, and the harsh landscape is dotted with salt flats and sand dunes. Another lodge and a few visitor services are also located there. In contrast, nearby Emigrant Canyon Road climbs up to the Charcoal Kilns and offers sweeping views of the snow capped Panamint Mountains.

Attractions

Stovepipe Wells Ranger Station

Accessible parking is available in front of the Stovepipe Wells Ranger Station, with ramp access up to the front door. This is the major information center for the area. There are no public restrooms, but visitors can pay entrance fees and pick up maps and a park newspaper there.

Mesquite Flat Sand Dunes

Mesquite Flat Sand Dunes

Although these sand dunes are visible from Stovepipe Wells, they are also worth a stop while traveling down Highway 190. Accessible parking is available next to the accessible vault toilets, and there's curb-cut access up to the interpretive panels on the other side of the parking lot. You can get a good view of the dunes from that spot; however there is a 250-foot hard-packed dirt trail that leads out to the brink of the dunes and offers a different perspective on the area. There's about a one-inch step down to the trail, and although there are a few small rocks here and there, they are pretty easy to dodge. This is one of the most accessible sand dune areas in the park.

Devils Cornfield

Located near the intersection of Highway 190 and Scotty's Castle Road, Devils Cornfield is easy to spot. There's no formal parking area for this stop, but there are paved pullouts on both sides of the road near an interpretative plaque that sheds some light on these unusual plants. Although the plants resemble bundled corn left to dry, they are actually arrowweed plants that have adapted to their harsh desert environment. The high winds in the area have scoured the sand away from the plant roots and left pedestals of dirt and exposed roots at their bases, thus giving them their strange haystack look.

Devils Cornfield

Trails

Salt Creek Boardwalk

One of the most accessible trails in the park, Salt Creek Boardwalk, is located at the end of a three-mile dirt road of off Highway 190, south of the Scotty's Castle Road intersection. And although this road usually closes after heavy rains it's passable in even low clearance vehicles when it's open. There's no striped parking area at the boardwalk, however the area is flat and it's easy to parallel park an adapted van there. There's also an accessible vault toilet and an accessible picnic table located near the parking area.

The half-mile round trip trail winds around Salt Creek, which is home to the indigenous pupfish. Although the creek dries up in the summer, you'll usually find water there from November through May. The lack of railings on the level boardwalk also affords wheelchair-users an unobstructed view of the surrounding landscape. It should also be noted that there is no shade in this area, so bring a hat, and visit early in the day if possible.

Salt Creek Boardwalk

Picnic Areas

Hells Gate

Located near the intersection of Mud Canyon and the Beatty Cutoff, this picnic area and information station makes for a good rest stop. There's accessible parking near the accessible vault toilet, and curb-cut access up to a shaded accessible picnic table with a nice badlands view. There's also an additional picnic table on the dirt, but it's not shaded. Visitors can also pay entrance fees at the automated kiosk, and pick up park information and maps.

Emigrant Picnic Area

Located at the intersection of Highway 190 and Emigrant Canyon Road, on the west side of the park, this small picnic area features parking in a level asphalt lot. There is one accessible picnic table on a dirt pad, but it's not shaded. There are restrooms at this stop but they all have at least one step up. There's also an old Civilian Conservation Corps building across the street that once housed a ranger station. Although it makes for a good photo op, there's also a step up to the front porch.

Hells Gate picnic area

Lodging

Stovepipe Wells Village Hotel

51880 Highway 190
Death Valley National Park, CA 92328
(760) 786-7090
www.deathvalleyhotels.com

This historic hotel, which sports a decidedly western theme, has been serving Death Valley visitors since 1926. Access improvements are continually added to this comfortable property; including a recently installed lowered check-in counter in the office. The staff is friendly, the rooms are comfortable, and you just can't beat the desert views. This 83-room hotel has two accessible rooms with roll-in showers, and two semi-accessible rooms with low-step showers.

Accessible parking is located in front of the gift shop with level access over to the registration desk, which is located behind the business center. The two accessible rooms are located a short walk away, near the pool and close to the restaurant and saloon. Accessible parking is also available in front of accessible rooms 49 and 50, with barrier-free access over to each room.

Room 50 at Stovepipe Wells Village Hotel

Bathroom in room 50 at Stovepipe Wells Village Hotel

Room 50 features wide doorways, lever handles, low-pile carpet, and barrier-free pathways throughout the unit. It's furnished with two 26-inch high open-frame full beds, with wheelchair access on all sides. Other furnishings include an easy chair, a chest of drawers, and a small refrigerator.

Room 49 at Stovepipe Wells Village Hotel

Bathroom in room 49 at Stovepipe Wells Village Hotel

The spacious bathroom includes a full five-foot turning radius, and is equipped with a large roll-in shower with grab bars, a handheld showerhead and a fold-down shower seat. Other access features include a toilet with grab bars on the back and left walls (as seated), and a roll-under sink.

Room 49 has the same basic access features, except that the toilet grab bars are located on the back and right walls (as seated). This room has a slightly different configuration, as the furniture is placed differently; however it still offers excellent pathway access.

Room 74, which is located on the other side of the complex may work for some slow walkers. Parking is available directly in front of the room, with barrier-free access to the front door. Access features include wide doorways, lever handles, low-pile carpet, and good pathway access throughout the unit.

Furnishings include a 26-inch high open-frame king-sized bed with wheelchair access on both sides, an easy chair, a chest of drawers and a refrigerator. There's also a back door that opens up to a shared back patio, and includes plenty of room for a wheelchair or scooter.

The bathroom features a low-step (two-inch) shower, a roll-under sink, and a toilet with grab bars on the back and left walls (as seated).

There's barrier-free access to all the public areas of the hotel, including the restaurants and the gift shop. Wi-Fi is available in the accessible business

Room 74 at Stovepipe Wells Village Hotel

Bathroom in room 74 at Stovepipe Wells Village Hotel

center, and although the signal is weak, it's good enough for e-mail. There's also barrier-free access to the swimming pool, which includes a portable wheelchair-lift. This rustic property captures the spirit of Death Valley and offers good wheelchair access.

Stovepipe Wells Village Hotel is open year-round.

Stovepipe Wells RV Park

Located behind the General Store this small RV park has 14 spaces with full hookups. There are no designated accessible spaces, but they are all located in a level area with nice mountain views. There are no picnic tables or grills in this campground. There also aren't any bathrooms or shower facilities; however guests receive a daily shower and pool pass to Stovepipe Wells Village Hotel, which is just across the street. The pool includes a wheelchair lift, and the shower houses feature level access, a large toilet stall without grab bars, some low-step showers and a large changing area. This bathroom setup will work for many slow walkers.

Stovepipe Wells RV Park is open year-round. Reservations can be made online at www.deathvalleyhotels.com, or by calling (760) 786-7090.

Stovepipe Wells Village RV Park

Stovepipe Wells Campground

Located behind the general store this NPS campground has tent sites and non-electric sites. There are no designated accessible campsites, but the area is level so the standard sites may work for many folks. There are no picnic tables or grills at the campsites. There is level access to the restrooms which have accessible stalls and roll-under sinks.

Stovepipe Wells Campground is open from mid-September to mid-May. Campsites are available on a walk-in basis.

Emigrant Campground

Located next to the Emigrant Picnic Area, there is no charge to camp at this tents only campground. There is no accessible parking area, but all of the spots are paved and level. The sites are pretty basic, and have level pads and standard picnic tables. Restrooms are available at the nearby picnic area; however they all have a step up into them. Water is also available at the picnic area.

Emigrant Campground is open year-round, and the campsites are available on a walk-in basis.

Dining

Badwater Saloon

Accessible parking is available near the hotel registration desk, and even though steps grace the front of the Badwater Saloon, there's also ramp access. Inside there's plenty of room to maneuver a wheelchair around the tables, and barrier-free access to the accessible restrooms. The wagon wheel chandeliers and the old mining implements that line the walls set the mood for this western themed watering hole. This casual eatery is open for lunch and dinner and the menu includes a good selection of sandwiches, wraps, soups, salads and appetizers. And of course, there's lots of beer on tap.

Toll Road Restaurant

Located next door to the Badwater Saloon, this restaurant also offers ramp access on the side. There's plenty of room to maneuver around the tables, and the accessible restrooms are shared with the Badwater Saloon. The restaurant offers breakfast favorites in the morning and soups, salads and hearty entrees at dinner time.

Services

Grocery Store ?, (General Store? Not online)

Accessible parking is located on the left side of the store, and there's a barrier-free path to the front door. Inside there's room to maneuver a wheelchair around the shelves, which are stocked with snacks, drinks, ready-made sandwiches, grocery items, books, souvenirs, camping supplies and firewood. Accessible restrooms are located on the right side of the building.

Gas Station

The gas station is located next to the store, and it offers level access to the pumps. It is open 24 hours for debit and credit card purchases.

Showers

Daily shower and pool passes to the facilities at Stovepipe Wells Village Hotel are available for $4 at the hotel registration desk. These passes are available to the general public and they include unlimited access to the pool and showers for the whole day. Visitors who purchase the passes are issued gate keys so they can come and go as they please. The pool includes a wheelchair lift, and the shower houses feature level access, a large toilet stall without grab bars, some low-step showers and a large changing area. This bathroom setup will work for many slow walkers.

Closed until 2023

Scotty's Castle

Elevation – 3,005 Feet

Located north of Stovepipe Wells, this section of the park is relatively remote. It's also an area that's prone to flooding after heavy rains; in fact Scotty's Castle was heavily damaged in 2015; and both the home and the road through Grapevine Canyon are still closed. Besides the famous desert domicile, there are also a few interesting geological features as well as a ranger station, campground and a picnic area there.

Attractions

Grapevine Ranger Station

This small information station is located near the turn-off to Mesquite Spring Campground on Scotty's Castle Road. There's accessible parking with curb-cut access up to the building, but this ranger station is usually unmanned. Maps and other park information are posted on the outside bulletin board. The restrooms at this stop are not wheelchair-accessible.

Scotty's Castle

Constructed in the 1920s by Chicago insurance magnate Albert Johnson, Scotty's Castle is a definite oasis in the desert. It was named after Walter Scott — also known as Death Valley Scotty — who made his living by convincing wealthy businessmen (including Johnson) to invest in his Death Valley gold mine. The mine never produced one ounce of ore, but Johnson forgave Scotty because the desert air cleared up his health problems. After Johnson built his palatial mansion Scotty became a permanent resident, and subsequently it became known as Scotty's Castle.

Scotty's Castle before the floods

Unfortunately Scotty's Castle received an estimated $47 million of da
from flooding that followed a torrential downpour in October 2015.
are currently underway and it's hoped that the landmark will be able to re-
open in late 2021, however that date is funding-dependent. Previously the
Scotty's Castle tour had stair lift access to the second floor, and alternative
accessible pathways for wheelchair-users; and it's expected that it will have
at least the same level of access when it reopens. Check the park website for
reopening updates.

Ubehebe Crater   *Paved road*

Located six miles from Scotty's Castle at the end of the park road, Ubehebe
Crater is definitely worth a stop when you are in this end of the park.
Accessible parking is located near the overlook, with curb-cut access over to
the interpretive panel. Created by a powerful volcanic steam explosion, the
massive crater is 600 feet deep and over a half-mile across. The trail around
the crater is not accessible due to loose soil and some steep climbs, but
there's good access to the level sidewalk along the rim near the parking area.
The drive up to the parking area is also quite scenic. You feel like you've
reached the top of the world when you arrive. It can also get quite windy up
there, so be sure to hang on to your hat.

Ubehebe Crater

Picnic Areas

Scotty's Castle Road Picnic Area

This small information station and picnic area is located near the intersection of Scotty's Castle Road and Highway 374. There's accessible parking near the accessible vault toilet, with curb-cut access over to a covered accessible picnic table. Another table is located in an open dirt area. There's also an automated kiosk to pay the park entrance fee, and a supply of park newspapers there. There's not much to this small stop, but the desert views are great, and the covered picnic table is a real plus.

Scotty's Castle Road Picnic Area

Panamint Springs

Elevation – 1,926 feet

L ocated on the west side of the park this area has an overlook that offers a nice view of colorful Rainbow Canyon. There's also a rustic resort that has a campground, gas station, restaurant and a general store. The resort has a hotel, but it doesn't have any accessible rooms. And as you make your way along Highway 190 up to Towne Pass, the windshield views keep getting better and better.

Attractions

Father Crowley Point

63 miles west of Furnace Creek Visitor Ct. 44 miles from Stovepipe wells (38 min)

The first developed facility on the west side of the park, Father Crowley Point is located just west of Panamint Springs. Named for the Padre of the Desert, this stop offers some excellent views of colorful Rainbow Canyon. There's accessible parking with curb-cut access up to a sidewalk and an interpretive panel about Rainbow Canyon. There's also barrier-free access to two accessible vault toilets near the interpretive panel. A short sidewalk

The view at Father Crowley Point

leads along the canyon over to a commemorative plaque dedicated to Father Crowley. There's a short dirt path that leads out to another canyon view, but it's a bit rocky and not accessible. Still the view is wonderful from the parking lot overlook. Go in the morning for the best color.

Lodging

Panamint Springs Campground

Located across the street from the Panamint Springs Grill, this campground is not a good choice for wheelchair-users. The dirt paths around the tent sites are level, but they are a bit rocky, and the restrooms are not accessible. Additionally the tent cabins all have a step up to them. This campground may suffice for visitors who have their own RV, and don't need to use the campground restrooms. Full hookups and dry sites are available. Panamint Springs Campground is open year-round. Reservations can be made by calling (775) 482-7680 or e-mailing reservations@panamintsprings.com. Information about the campground is available at www.panamintsprings.com, however reservations cannot be made online.

Dining

Panamint Springs Grill

Although the food is good and the service is friendly at this remote outpost, the access leaves a little to be desired. There's no striped parking in the dirt parking lot, however it is level. The front entrance to the restaurant has several steps, however there is a level path on the right side that winds around back to the porch. From there it's a short walk to the front door. The porch has a flagstone path that is a bit bumpy, but it is level. The restrooms have narrow doorways and a six-inch step up to them, so they won't work for wheelchair-users. There were however, a good number of slow walkers that seemed to navigate around the obstacles without much trouble. Inside there's plenty of room to maneuver a wheelchair around the tables, and in good weather you can also dine on the porch. The grill offers a Continental breakfast buffet in the morning, and soups, salads, sandwiches, burgers and appetizers the rest of the day. It also has a full service bar.

Services

General Store

The General Store is located next to the Panamint Springs Grill. Like the rest of the facilities at Panamint City, parking is available in an unstriped dirt lot. There's ramp access up to the General Store, with plenty of room to maneuver a wheelchair around the shelves inside. There is also an accessible restroom inside the store, but the ice cream case partially blocks the access aisle, so it won't do for large wheelchairs. That said, the store has the most accessible restroom in Panamint City. The store offers snack items, food, drinks, camping supplies, souvenirs and firewood.

Gas Station

The gas station is located in front of the General Store. There's level access to the pumps, but customers must pay for their purchases inside the store. The gas station is open 24 hours a day.

Interesting junk at the Panamint Springs Gas Station

Death Valley Resources

Death Valley National Park
(760) 786-3200
www.nps.gov/deva
www.facebook.com/DeathValleyNPS
www.facebook.com/DeathValleyRoadConditions

Xanterra Travel Collection (in-park concessionaire)
(800) 236-7916
www.oasisatdeathvalley.com
www.facebook.com/oasisatdeathvalley

Ortega National Parks (in-park concessionaire)
(760) 786-7090
www.deathvalleyhotels.com

Gateway Community Attractions

Ruins in the ghost town of Rhyolite

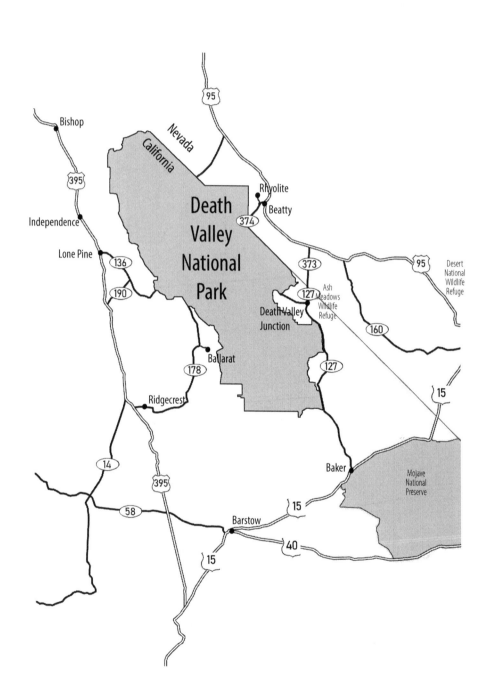

Because of its remote location, Death Valley is a prime candidate for a road trip. And the good news is, no matter what direction you come from, there are plenty of interesting attractions to enjoy along the way. Additionally, since the landscape and geology varies greatly in the areas bordering the park, it's a good idea to leave by a different exit to get the most out of your visit. And although some of the country surrounding the park is certainly pretty rugged, these attractions are good choices for wheelchair-users and slow walkers.

East

The communities along the eastern edge of the park are few and far between. That said the area boasts some stunning natural attractions as well as a good sprinkling of ghost towns. It's a favorite spot for photographers, and a good choice for anyone who wants to dodge the maddening crowds. And if you'd like to hit another national park on your way home, Great Basin National Park is just a 5.5-hour drive away, via a stretch of the loneliest road in America.

Las Vegas

Elevation 2,500 feet

Desert National Wildlife Refuge

16001 Corn Creek Road
Las Vegas, NV 89124
(702) 879-6110
www.fws.gov/refuge/Desert

A recommended stop if you're headed to Death Valley from Las Vegas, this refuge is located off of Highway 95 on Corn Creek Road. It's about a half-hour drive from downtown Las Vegas.

Accessible parking is available in front — and it's even shaded — with barrier-free access over to the visitor center. Inside there's plenty of room to maneuver a wheelchair around the information desk, bookstore and interpretive exhibits. There's also level access to the auditorium, where a short film about the refuge is shown throughout the day. Accessible restrooms are located in front of the building, and there's a shaded area with a few tables near the entrance.

Desert National Wildlife Refuge

There are four trails through the preserve, three of which are wheelchair-accessible. The Jackrabbit Loop, which is located next to the visitor center, is a short .1-mile loop that offers an introduction to the flora and fauna found in the area. It's level and includes a combination of hard-packed dirt surfaces covered in decomposed gravel, along with some concrete sidewalk sections. About midway along the loop the trail branches off to the .4-mile Bighorn Loop, which is equally accessible. Alternatively you can continue along the Jackrabbit Loop if you'd just like a short walk. Both of these trails were resurfaced in 2019 to repair storm damage.

The Coyote Loop begins just past the pond, and continues along Corn Creek. This .3-mile trail is mostly level, and offers a good opportunity to get a close look at the avian residents of the refuge. There's also a short accessible trail up to the Railroad Tie Cabin near the beginning of the Coyote Loop. This unique structure was built with abandoned railroad ties in the early 1920s. A small shaded picnic area with a few accessible tables is located near the cabin. And don't miss the refugium, an aquarium-like exhibit that's filled with what's believed to be the remaining population of Pahrump Poolfish. It's also located near the historic cabin.

All in all the refuge makes a nice stop for a picnic lunch, and it's a good place to stretch your legs and get a close look at Mother Nature.

Amargosa Valley

Elevation 2,210

Ash Meadows National Wildlife Refuge

610 East Springs Meadows Road
Armargosa Valley, NV 89020
(775) 372-5435
www.fws.gov/refuge/Ash_Meadows

Located off of Highway 373 between Highway 95 and Death Valley Junction, this refuge also makes a good stop on the way to the park from Las Vegas. And since you can enter the refuge on one side and exit on another, you don't have to backtrack.

There's accessible shaded parking near the visitor center with barrier-free access to the front door. Inside there's plenty of room to maneuver a wheelchair around the interpretive exhibits, bookstore and information desk. There's level access and wheelchair seating in the auditorium, where a film about the refuge is shown. Accessible restrooms are located near the shaded accessible picnic area on the side of the building.

An accessible .9-mile loop boardwalk begins at the back door and leads

Crystal Springs Boardwalk in Ash Meadows National Wildlife Refuge

across the alkali flats to Crystal Spring. It offers some excellent mountain views, and it's not uncommon to spot a variety of birds, including Wilson's Warblers and Anna's Hummingbirds, along the boardwalk. The spring is home to Armargosa Pupfish and Western Mosquitofish, as well as a decent population of American Bullfrogs. And the Green-Winged Teals seem to be everywhere.

There is another accessible boardwalk a short drive from the visitor center on Longstreet Road, but that road is not suitable for low clearance vehicles. Devils Hole, which is a remote unit of Death Valley National Park, is also located in the refuge; however there's nothing of note to see there. It's home to the once endangered Devils Hole Pupfish, but since these fish live deep in the cavern waters they are not visible from the surface. An inaccessible trail leads over to the unit, which is surrounded by a chain link fence, so it's really not worth the drive.

The Point of Rocks Boardwalk, is most definitely worth a stop though. It's located south of the visitor center off of Spring Meadows Road. There's accessible parking near the accessible vault toilets, and level access to a shaded accessible picnic area. An accessible boardwalk begins near the picnic area and leads out to Kings Pool and over to the amphitheater and viewing area at the end of the line. It's about a .7-mile round trip walk. Pupfish are usually visible in the spring, and there's also a variety of avian

Point of Rocks Boardwalk in Ash Meadows National Wildlife Refuge

life at this site. And you'll probably see more than a few lizards scamper across the boardwalk along the way.

After you complete your hike, make a left on Spring Meadows Road and exit the refuge at the South Entrance. This road is sometimes flooded after storms, but it's usually passable in dry weather. From the South Entrance, it's about a six-mile drive to Death Valley Junction, where you can connect with Highway 190 and enter the park.

Death Valley Junction

Elevation 2,000 Feet

Amargosa Opera House, Hotel and Cafe

608 Highway 127
Death Valley Junction, CA 92328
(760) 852-4441
www.amargosacafe.org

Once a bustling community of 300 during the borax mining boom, Death Valley Junction — which was originally named Amargosa — is little more

Amargosa Hotel at Death Valley Junction

than a shadow if its former self. New York City ballet dancer Marta Becket discovered the ghost town when she had a flat tire on her way to Death Valley in the late 1960s. She later rented the dorm and recreation hall from the Pacific Coast Borax Company, and magically transformed them into a hotel and opera house. She painted murals throughout the hotel, and even painted an audience on the walls of the opera house. On February 10, 1968 she debuted her one-woman performance to the hand-painted audience. Shortly thereafter she was profiled in some popular magazines and people traveled for miles to see Becket perform in this unique venue.

Becket passed away in 2017, but occasional guest performances are still held at the Amargosa Opera House. There's level access to the venue, and tours are also available upon request. Make sure and stop in the hotel lobby — which has a level entrance — to see Becket's colorful murals. Some of Becket's costumes are also on display in a building across the highway from the opera house. There's level access around the building, and the items can be seen through the windows.

Unfortunately the Amargosa Cafe has a serious eight-inch step up at the front entrance, but if you can manage that, they are usually open from Friday to Sunday for breakfast and lunch. Alternatively you can pack a picnic and enjoy lunch at the picnic table near the hotel entrance.

Beatty

Elevation 3,307 Feet

Beatty Historical Museum

417 Main Street
Beatty, NV 89003
(775) 553-2303
www.beattymuseum.org

Located along the main drag, this local museum is appropriately housed in a historic church. There's accessible parking near the entrance, with ramp access up to the museum. Inside there's plenty of room to maneuver a wheelchair around the exhibits that include everything from old telegraph equipment, furniture and china, to a sewing machine collection, farm implements and even an organ that was used in Scotty's Castle in the 1960s. Add in a large collection of photographs of Beatty in the boom days, and you get a real feel

Beatty Historical Museum

for what it was like back when the mines were active. The volunteers on duty are happy to field questions about Death Valley and the surrounding area, and there's even a Death Valley exhibit in the museum. Although it doesn't look like much on the outside, it's a must-stop on the way to the park.

Goldwell Open Air Museum

1 Golden Street
Beatty, NV 89003
(702) 870-9946
goldwellmuseum.org

Located on the way to Rhyolite, this unique open-air sculpture installation is definitely worth a stop. From Beatty, head west on Highway 374 for about four miles, then turn right on Rhyolite Road. Take the first left on the road – look for a miner with a penguin – and you've found the museum. It's really pretty hard to miss. There's parking in a level dirt area, and usually there's plenty of room for an adapted van. A small information center that's ramped in the back is located nearby. The information center is open periodically, but even if it's closed you can still pick up a brochure about the artwork.

The sculptures are dotted throughout the desert, with mostly level paths covered in gravel leading out and around them. That said, you can get a

Penguin and Miner sculpture at the Goodwell Open Air Musrum

good look at the bulk of them from the information center, so it's worth a stop even if you can't negotiate the paths. The sculptures range from a ghostly interpretation of the Last Supper, to the more traditional Tribute to Shorty Harris, a legendary Rhyolite prospector. And there are even a few pieces that visitors can sit or lean on, and snap a selfie or two.

Rhyolite Ghost Town

Beatty, NV 89003

Now a ghost town, Rhyolite was established in 1904, after Shorty Harris discovered gold nearby. The town, which is named for the silica-rich volcanic rock in the area, thrived while the Montgomery Shoshone mine was in full operation; and at one time it had an estimated population of 5,000 to 8,000. By 1910 gold production had dropped dramatically, and people began to move away; and by 1920 the population dwindled to just 14. Today the historic Las Vegas & Tonopah Depot and Tom Kelly's Bottle House still stand, but for the most part the rest of the town is in ruins. You can get a good windshield view of the remnants of the school, bank and general store from the road, and there are plenty of level spots to pull over to get a closer look. Accessible vault toilets are located at the end of the road, and there's even an accessible picnic table in front of the depot. Located just four miles west of Beatty, Rhyolite makes a good stop on the way to or from Death Valley.

Tom Kelly's Bottle House
Beatty, NV 89003

This iconic structure, which was erected in 1906, is one of the first things you spot as you enter Rhyolite. Tom Kelly built this masterpiece from 51,000 beer bottles, adobe and mud; and since there were some 50 bars in town, there was never a shortage of building materials. As for Kelly's motivation and reasoning for his chosen medium — he often said that it was easier to build a home from beer bottles than it was to mill lumber from the native Joshua Trees. Interestingly enough, Kelly never lived in the house, but instead raffled it off. Today, accessible parking is available on a cement pad in the dirt lot, with a level sidewalk from the parking space over to the house. Although the house sits behind a fence to protect it from vandals, the gate is sometimes open; however even if it's closed you can still get an excellent gander at Kelly's creation from the sidewalk near the entrance.

Tom Kelly's Bottle House

Highway 395 cuts through the eastern Sierras and offers a scenic approach to the park from Northern California. The landscape transitions from the snow capped Minarets in the north to a high desert landscape near the end of the route. And although there's no shortage of great windshield views along the way, these attractions in Bishop, Lone Pine, Ridgecrest and Trona are definitely worth a stop.

Bishop

Elevation 4,500 Feet

Laws Railroad Museum

Silver Canyon Road
Bishop (Laws), CA 93514
(760) 873-5950
www.lawsmuseum.org

Located about four miles from the center of Bishop in the former rail town of Laws, this open-air museum offers a primer on local railroad history, and presents a glimpse into pioneer life in the Owens Valley. During the late 1800s the Carson & Colorado Railroad ran through the town, which at one time supported two general stores, a rooming house, an eating house, a hotel, a pool hall, a dance hall and all the other trappings of the old west.

Sadly when the local mines closed, and trucking became more economical than shipping goods by rail, this once thriving community died. Subsequently the railroad donated the museum grounds, historic buildings and rolling stock to the city of Bishop, and shortly thereafter the museum was established. Today, more historic buildings have been moved to the site, and most are filled with goods from days-gone-by. From the photographer's studio, general store and post office, to the dentist's office, fire station and even an old Wells Fargo building, there's something for just about everyone at this fascinating railroad museum.

Parking is available in an unstriped asphalt lot across the street from the museum. From there it's just a short level walk to the reception center, which offers ramp access. Most of the buildings have ramped or level access, and there are also level brick and dirt paths around them. Level boardwalks connect some buildings, while others may have a step or two. There's also a large collection of vintage farm equipment in a level dirt area, as well as a 20 Mule Team Borax wagon on display in the barn (compliments of the Death Valley Conservancy and the American Mule Museum). Locomotive Number 9 – a 1909 ten-wheel Baldwin – is also prominently displayed next to the original 1883 depot.

There are family restrooms near the fire house, and visitors are invited to bring a lunch to enjoy at one of the accessible picnic tables in a level dirt area near the train. All in all, the access is pretty good for a historic site. The Laws Railroad Museum is just a short hop off of Highway 395, but it's an interesting detour on the way to or from Death Valley – especially for railroad buffs.

The depot at Laws Railroad Museum

Mule Days

Bishop, CA 95313
(760) 872-4263
www.muledays.org

If you happen to be in the area on Memorial Day Weekend, then make plans to attend some of the Mule Days events. At the top of the list is the Main Street parade, which takes place on Saturday morning. Billed as the largest non-motorized parade in America, this festive event features mule teams, horses, wagons, bands and lots of mules with costumed riders. And in keeping with tradition, there's usually a 20-mule team wagon in the mix. Accessible parking for the parade is available in front of the Bishop Dog Park, but it's best to ask the officer at the Main Street road block to direct you to other accessible parking areas.

The bulk of the other events take place at the Tri-County Fairgrounds over the next two days. The arena events resemble something akin to a mule rodeo, where the packers show off their skills. The whole event is steeped in tradition, as mule packers are a fixture in the Sierras for back country camping, hunting and rescue operations. There are no money prizes for the winners at Mule Days, but the bragging rights are huge.

Accessible parking is available in the fairgrounds parking lot, and a paved

20 Mule Team in the Mule Days Parade in Bishop, California

level pathway leads from the parking area, around the mule barns to the grandstand. Accessible seating for up to two people is available in Box 1 in the grandstand, and for groups of three or more in the first rows of Sections A and E. It's best to call and order your tickets as far in advance as possible. Additionally, it's extremely important to specify that you need accessible seating when you place your order.

Independence

Elevation 3,727 Feet

Manzanar

5001 Highway 395
Independence, CA 93526
(760) 878-2194 ext. 3310
www.nps.gov/manz

Manzanar National Historic Site, which is located mid-way between Independence and Lone Pine on Highway 395, is a required stop for anyone interested in World War II history. This former relocation center interred over 10,000 Japanese American citizens after the attack on Pearl Harbor.

Cemetery at Manzanar interment camp

There's ramp access up to the auditorium, which now houses the visitor center; and barrier-free access around the interpretive exhibits and over to the theater, where a film about the site is shown. Visitors can view the rest of the camp on a 3.2-mile self-drive tour of the complex. Although the buildings were dismantled shortly after WWII ended, the sentry post, guard towers, historic orchards, rock gardens and the cemetery are still intact. Additionally, Block 14, which houses two reconstructed barracks, is located next to the visitor center. There's ramp access up to the barracks, which offers some insight on the harsh living conditions at the camp. It's a sobering site, and a reminder of a dark period in US history.

Eastern California Museum

155 N. Grant Street
Independence, CA 93526
(760) 878-0258
www.inyocounty.us/ecmsite

For another perspective on Manzanar, be sure and stop by the Eastern California Museum in Independence. There is accessible parking in front and level access to this small museum, which boasts a substantial collection of historic Manzanar photographs, and a replica of a typical barracks apartment. The bulk of the museum is dedicated to one of the

Baskets in the Eastern California Museum

largest collections of Owens Valley Paiute-Shoshone and Death Valley Panamint-Shoshone basketry in the nation. Ornamental and functional baskets, along with cradleboards, projectile points, bows and arrows, and rare examples of Paiute beadwork are included in the extensive exhibit. The collection includes over 400 baskets and nearly 100 other related artifacts, and is housed in 14 large display cases. Other ongoing exhibits highlight the history, geology and people of the area. Best of all, there's no admission charge to this excellent local museum.

Lone Pine

Elevation 3,727 Feet

Museum of Western Film History

701 S. Main
Lone Pine, CA 93545
(760) 876-9909
www.museumofwesternfilmhistory.org

The Museum of Western Film History presents a comprehensive history of films that were shot in the area. There's accessible parking in front of the museum with level access to the front door. Inside, there's plenty of room to navigate a wheelchair around the large collection of movie memorabilia from movies shot in the Alabama Hills. From saddles and posters, to costumes, props and even a stagecoach, there's a lot to see in this excellent museum. There's also ramped access to the movie theater, where a short introductory film is shown. It's the perfect primer for a drive along Movie Road.

Alabama Hills Movie Road Tour

Whitney Portal Road
Lone Pine, CA 93545
www.lonepinechamber.org
(760) 876-4444

Located in Lone Pine just off Highway 395, Whitney Portal Road was once known as Movie Road, because so many films were shot there. Starting in 1919 *The Round-Up* was filmed in the Alabama Hills, and over the years all the big western actors — including Tom Mix, Gene Autry and John Wayne — shot on location there. And although the scenery was perfect for

Mount Whitney viewed from Movie Road

westerns, *The Twilight Zone*, *Star Trek 5* and *Tremors* were also filmed there. There are a number of interpretive plaques along Movie Road that point out the filming locations; and although there's no accessible parking along the route, there are level spaces to pull over near the filming sites.

Ridgecrest

Elevation 2,290 Feet

Maturango Museum

100 E. Las Flores Avenue
Ridgecrest, CA 93555
(760) 375-6900
www.maturango.org

The Maturango Museum highlights the natural and cultural history of the Northern Mojave Desert. There's accessible parking in front, with level access to the entrance, and barrier-free access throughout the museum. Exhibits offer a good overview of the flora and fauna of the area, and include displays on the Coso Petroglyphs and Walker Pass. The museum gift shop also serves as an information center for Death Valley and the

The Gladys Merrick Garden at the Maturango Museum

Northern Mojave Desert, so it's a good place to stock up on maps or ask for directions. Outside, the Gladys Merrick Garden features hard-packed dirt trails that wind around vintage mining equipment, a labyrinth, some standard picnic tables and a nice collection of desert plants.

China Lake Museum

130 E. Las Flores Avenue
Ridgecrest, CA 93555
(760) 677-2866
www.chinalakemuseum.org

Located next door to the Maturango Museum, the China Lake Museum offers a fascinating overview of some of the civilian-military projects that were developed at nearby China Lake Naval Air Weapons Station (NAWS). Opened in 1943 as a sister base to Los Alamos, the largely civilian NAWS provided essential research, development and testing of the Fat Man atomic bomb, as well as a substantial number of military missiles.

Accessible parking is located in front of the museum, with barrier-free access to the entrance. Inside there's plenty of room to navigate a wheelchair or scooter around the exhibits, and through the military-themed gift shop. Accessible family restrooms are located near the gift shop.

The exhibits chronicle the history of the NAWS, from the stark living conditions at its inception, through the testing and development of air weapons from World War II to the present day. Armaments developed and tested at the China Lake NAWS include the Sidewinder, Polaris and Shrike missiles. There's also some interesting footage of the test detonations as well as videos of the base in the early days.

Outside there's a level sidewalk around the military aircraft on display, including a F-18A Hornet. The museum was relocated from the base in 2018, and expansion plans include the addition of another wing and a hangar. Future additions are expected to be extremely accessible, as it's a favorite stop for veterans, and the volunteers and staff are extremely conscious of access needs. The China Lake Museum is a must-see for anyone interested in military history, especially the Manhattan Project.

Displays in the China Lake Museum

Trona

Elevation 1,800 Feet

Ballarat Ghost Town

Ballarat Road
Trona, CA 93592

Located 45 miles east of Ridgecrest, between Trona and Stovepipe Wells, this former boom town was founded after gold was discovered at the nearby Radcliff Mine in 1897. There's a graded dirt road that leads from Highway 178 to the town site, and although it's passable in a low clearance vehicle in dry weather, it's also prone to flooding when it rains. There's no designated parking, but there's plenty of room to pull over on the dirt and explore the area. A nearby sign welcomes visitors and reminds folks, "You learn nothing sitting in your car." There's plenty of room to wander around the level town site, which is more accurately described as a ruins. There are a few buildings still standing, including the jail and a trading post, but other than that it's just you and the desert. Still it makes a pleasant scenic drive, and there's even a picnic shelter at the far end of town where you can enjoy a secluded lunch break.

Ruins in Ballarat ghost town

The Southern route to the park winds through the Los Angeles metropolitan area before it crosses the wide open expanse of Interstate 15 between Barstow and Baker. The desert scenery is beautiful, and there are a few fun and kitschy attractions to stop at along the way.

Barstow

Elevation 2,175 Feet

Western America Railroad Museum

685 N. First Avenue
Barstow, CA 92312
(760) 256-9276
www.barstowrailmuseum.org

Opened in 1911, Casa Del Desierto was considered the crown jewel of the infamous Harvey House chain. Renovated and reopened in the mid-1900s, today this historic building is home to two transportation museums.

Casa Del Desierto

Located at the eastern end of the complex, the excellent Western America Railroad Museum is a must-see for railroad buffs. The museum's collection is comprehensive — some claim it borders on eclectic — while a cadre of enthusiastic volunteers eagerly await the opportunity to share their collective railroad knowledge with visitors.

Access is excellent at the museum too, with accessible parking in the adjacent lot and level access to the front door. Inside there's plenty of room to maneuver a wheelchair through the galleries which are filled to the brim with railroad memorabilia. Exhibits include everything from railroad tools and machines, to vintage schedules, uniforms, dinnerware and signs. And then there's the model railroad.

Don't miss the extensive Gustafson collection of railroad date nails. These nails were stamped with the date, then hammered into the rails for maintenance record purposes. Railroad crews ceased using the nails in 1969, and today computers keep track of the maintenance records. This extensive collection includes nails from all 50 states, which date back to the late 1800s. It's an interesting slice of railroad history.

There's also a nice collection of rolling stock out in the yard, with level access around the cars. Highlights include an Atchison, Topeka and Santa Fe caboose and diesel engine, a 1968 Cline wheel truck, and a Union Pacific caboose. There's also a large Atchison, Topeka and Santa Fe horse car, that was used to transport race horses and their owners across the country. And although the cars themselves do not offer wheelchair access, most of them are better admired from afar.

Barstow Route 66 Mother Road Museum

681 N. First Avenue
Barstow, CA 92311
(760) 255-1890
www.route66museum.org

The equally impressive Barstow Route 66 Mother Road Museum is located next to the Western America Railroad Museum. And although rail and automobile travel may seem an unlikely mix, many cross-country highways paralleled the rail lines; in fact, the original alignment of Route 66 ran right next to Casa Del Desierto.

Known as the Mother Road, Route 66 got its official numerical designation in 1926. The 2,448-mile route ran from Chicago to Los Angeles, and was comprised of existing roads in the eight states it traversed. Dust Bowl

Inside the Barstow Route 66 Mother Road Museum

immigrants headed west on the road in the 1930s, and as the trucking industry grew, so did the traffic on this popular roadway. After WWII, people flocked to Route 66 to "get their kicks" and stop at kitschy roadside attractions, diners, auto courts and motels along the way. Unfortunately the popularity of the Mother Road led to its ultimate demise, as the narrow lanes and outdated features were unable to handle the increased capacity. By 1970, nearly all segments of this once popular road were bypassed by a more modern four-lane highway.

But Route 66 history lives on in this nostalgic Barstow museum. There's level access to the building, and room enough to maneuver a wheelchair around most of the exhibits inside. From old photos, gas pumps, road signs and even a few cars you might have seen along the Mother Road, this fun museum is jam packed with Route 66 memorabilia. And if you'd like to take a slice of nostalgia home with you, there's also a small gift shop. It's really a great stop, especially if you plan to explore the remaining stretches of Route 66 in your future travels.

Baker

Mojave National Preserve

Zzyzx Road
Kelebaker Road
Baker, CA 92309
(760) 252-6100
www.nps.gov/moja

Located between Los Angeles and Las Vegas, the Mojave National Preserve is home to a multitude of natural wonders, from sand dunes and cinder cone volcanoes, to Joshua Tree forests and colorful wildflower patches. Although it's not possible to explore the entire 1.6-million acre preserve on a jaunt from Los Angeles to Death Valley, two sections — which are accessible from Interstate 15 — make for a scenic detour on the way to the national park.

The first area is located 60 miles east of Barstow — just look for the turnoff for Zzyzx Road. Although the odd name appears to just be a jumble of letters, the moniker was intentionally created by Curtis Howe Springer — a radio host and con man extraordinaire. He named the road — and his Zzyzx Mineral Springs Resort — with the last letters of the alphabet so he could hawk them with the tag line, "the last word in health". Sadly the resort didn't

Mineral Springs Resort

have hot springs either — he faked those by using a boiler to heat the pools around the resort.

Today Springer is only a memory in Zzyzx. The property is now home to the California State University Desert Studies Center; but visitors are welcome to walk around the property as long as they don't disturb the students.

The five-mile road to the former resort is mostly paved, and it passes by now dry Soda Lake before it dead ends in Zzyzx. There's accessible parking in a gravel lot near the Orientation Center, and curb-cut access up to the adjacent accessible vault toilets. And that's pretty much it for creature comforts.

There is however, a nice quarter-mile trail around Lake Tuendae, which is located behind the Desert Studies Center. From the parking area, go past the picnic area and take a right on the paved road, then take a left on the hard-packed dirt trail that leads over to the lake. The trail is level, and certainly doable in a wheelchair. It's an excellent place for desert birding, and there are a number of interpretive signs along the lakeside trail. And if you'd like to stop for lunch here, at least once of the standard picnic tables in the parking lot has room for a wheelchair to squeeze in on the end.

The other area in the preserve worth a stop is Kelso Depot. From Interstate 15 head south on Kelebaker Road, and continue on through the desert for

The Kelso Deoot

34 miles until you reach the historic site. You really can't miss it — it's the only thing for miles.

Built in 1924, Kelso Depot also contained sleeping quarters for employees as well as a restaurant. The Los Angeles & Salt Lake Railroad constructed the facility in order to compete with the popular Harvey Houses that the Santa Fe Railroad operated. Kelso Depot was upscale for the time, and it even had a billiard room and a library. The depot ceased functioning in 1962, although the restaurant remained open until 1985. Today it houses the visitor center for the Mojave National Preserve.

Accessible parking is located in front of the depot, with level access over to the visitor center and the nearby accessible restrooms. Inside there's barrier-free access throughout the facility, which includes interpretive exhibits about the Mojave National Preserve. Additionally the baggage room, ticket office and two dormitory rooms are furnished as they would have been in the 1920s. Unfortunately the visitor center is only open from Thursday to Monday, but even if it's closed you can still get a gander at the lunch counter, vintage desks and old equipment through the large front windows.

After you've had your fill of railroad history, just backtrack to the interstate and continue on to Death Valley.

Baker Thermometer

72157 Baker Boulevard
Baker, CA 92309
(760) 733-4747
www.worldstallestthermometer.com

Located in the middle of Baker, this infamous thermometer is worth a quick stop on the way to Death Valley. The brainchild of local businessman Willis Herron, the 134-foot tall thermometer was constructed in 1990, as a tribute to the record high temperature in the US — 134 degrees in Death Valley. Unfortunately Herron didn't account for the high winds in the area in his original plans, and as a result a strong gust brought the monument down, smashing a nearby gift shop that was under construction.

Undaunted, Herron rebuilt the thermometer, and filled the second model with concrete to keep it steady. And although the thermometer was shut down for a while after Herron's death, today it's up and running again. It's easy to find too — just take the Baker exit on Interstate 15 and follow the main drag until you see it on the south side of the street. To be honest, you can see it towering over the hamlet long before you even reach the freeway exit.

Accessible parking is available near the newly constructed gift shop, with barrier-free access to the thermometer, picnic tables and a few outside exhibits. There's level access to the adjacent gift shop which has snacks, souvenirs and accessible restrooms. And don't miss the photos on the back wall that illustrate the construction of the original thermometer, as well as its untimely demise.

The Baker Thermometer

Unfortunately it's difficult to get a good photo of the massive thermometer from the gift shop. That said there's an excellent vantage point next door — in the Del Taco parking lot – where you can easily get the whole thermometer in the photo. Accessible parking is available in the parking lot, and it's a nice level roll over to the far end, where you'll get a good view of the thermometer. And if the thermometer tops 100 — as it often does — you may just want to wander into the Del Taco for a nice cold drink.

Access
Resources

Artists Drive in Death Valley National Park

Emerging Horizons

www.EmergingHorizons.com

Your one-stop accessible travel resource.

- Destinations
- Lodging Options
- Tour Companies
- Travel News
- Trails & Recreation
- Travel Tips

Barrier-Free National Parks

www.barrierfreenationalparks.com

Access information on some of America's top national parks.

- Insider Tips
- Resources
- Suggested Itineraries
- Access Photos

Barrier-Free Travel
Yosemite, Sequoia and Kings Canyon National Parks
for Wheelers and Slow Walkers

By Candy B. Harrington

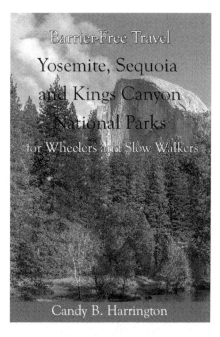

This indispensable guidebook includes detailed access information that will help wheelchair-users and slow walkers find an accessible room and build a barrier-free itinerary in Central California's top three national parks. Along with updated information about accessible trails, boardwalks, viewpoints, museums and picnic areas, this helpful resource also includes detailed access evaluations and photographs of 33 properties in and near the parks. And if you'd like to sleep under the stars, barrier-free campsites are also noted. Add in helpful details about the location of local airports, and the availability of accessible shuttles, public transportation and van rentals, and you've got all the information you need to get to and around the parks. Top it off with information on accessible bus tours, ranger programs, wheelchair and handcycle rentals and you have a must-have resource for wheelchair-users, stroller parents or anybody who just needs to take things a little slower.

www.barrierfreeyosemite.com

Barrier-Free Travel
The Grand Canyon
for Wheelers and Slow Walkers

By Candy B. Harrington

Penned by accessible travel expert Candy B. Harrington, this guidebook offers hard-to-find access information that will help wheelchair-users and slow walkers plan the ultimate road trip to Grand Canyon National Park. It offers detailed access information about trails and attractions in Grand Canyon National Park, as well as access details about lodging and attractions in gateway cities and Grand Canyon West. Accessible lodging choices, restaurants and attractions along Arizona's Interstate 40 and Route 66 are also noted. Information on accessible transfers from area airports and Amtrak stations, and details about nearby accessible van rentals are included. A must-read if the Grand Canyon is on your bucket list.

www.barrierfreegrandcanyon.com

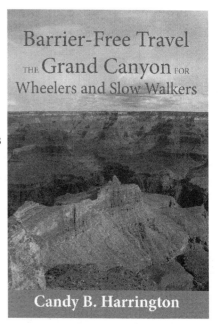

Barrier-Free Travel
National Park Lodges
for Wheelers and Slow Walkers

By Candy B. Harrington

The perfect guide for a national park road trip, *Barrier-Free Travel; National Park Lodges for Wheelers and Slow Walkers* includes detailed access information on 52 national park lodges throughout the mainland US. This essential resource also contains photos of the accessible rooms — including the bathrooms — and mentions often overlooked access details, such as bed heights. Information about accessible facilities, trails and attractions in the featured parks is also included, as is a "Don't Miss This" and an "Insider Tips" section. Add in information about accessible train, trolley, boat and bus tours, plus details on the best scenic drives and windshield views, and you have a comprehensive national park resource for wheelchair-users and slow walkers.

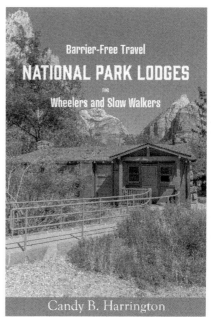

www.BFNationalParkLodges.com

Barrier-Free Travel
Yosemite, Sequoia and Kings Canyon National Parks
for Wheelers and Slow Walkers

By Candy B. Harrington

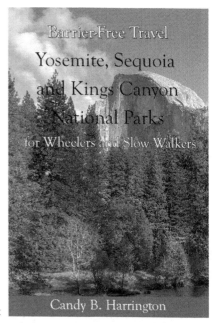

This indispensable guidebook includes detailed access information that will help wheelchair-users and slow walkers find an accessible room and build a barrier-free itinerary in Central California's top three national parks. Along with updated information about accessible trails, boardwalks, viewpoints, museums and picnic areas, this helpful resource also includes detailed access evaluations and photographs of 33 properties in and near the parks. And if you'd like to sleep under the stars, barrier-free campsites are also noted. Add in helpful details about the location of local airports, and the availability of accessible shuttles, public transportation and van rentals, and you've got all the information you need to get to and around the parks. Top it off with information on accessible bus tours, ranger programs, wheelchair and handcycle rentals and you have a must-have resource for wheelchair-users, stroller parents or anybody who just needs to take things a little slower.

www.barrierfreeyosemite.com

Barrier-Free Travel
Glacier, Yellowstone and Grand Teton National Parks
for Wheelers and Slow Walkers

By Candy B. Harrington

Penned by accessible travel expert Candy B. Harrington, this access guide includes detailed information about accessible trails, picnic areas, lodging options and attractions in Glacier, Yellowstone and Grand Teton National Parks. This handy resource features access details and photos of over 40 lodging options, including all in-park lodgings, as well as gateway city offerings. Details on accessible bus and boat tours, and shuttle service to, from and in the parks are also included. Top it off with information on recent access upgrades, barrier-free camping, and Amtrak, airport and accessible van rental details, and you have a one-stop national park resource. This guide will help you find an accessible room that works for you, and plan a accessible itinerary based on your abilities, to these three favorite national parks.

www.barrierfreeyellowstone.com

✓ Zabriskie Point (paved)
✓ Badwater Basin (salt flats)
✓ Crater (ubehebe) p51
✓ Devil's Golf Course (salt crystals)
✓ Artist's Road
✓ Dante's view?
✗ The Racetrack (moving rocks)
(83 miles from Furnace creek
on rough dirt roads)

✓ Twenty mile Team Canyon
←(dirt road 2.7 miles one-way Rd)
(just s. of Zabriskie Pt)

✓ Salt creek boardwalk (p 41)
Badwater mudflats (not on park map)
(mud flats on both sides of Bad H₂0 Rd)

Made in the USA
Las Vegas, NV
08 October 2021